O M Gee Good!
Instant Pot® Meals
Plant-Based & Oil Free

Jill McKeever

MW01044537

O M Gee Good! Instant Pot® Recipes, Plant-Based & Oil-free
Copyright © 2015 by Jill McKeever
Published by Jill McKeever
Photography by Jill McKeever
Cover by Jill McKeever

ISBN# 978-0-9851248-2-3

All rights reserved. No part of this book may be used or reproduced
in any manner whatsoever without written permission.

Instant Pot® is the registered trademark of Double Insight Inc.

Book Reviews from Fans

"I purchased an ipot last month when Amazon had them on sale. I just started using it this past week. I happened to stumble upon one of your videos as I was searching youtube for recipes, and now my life has changed forever. I downloaded your new cookbook last night. Love your sense of humor and your sense of taste. ;)" —**Pamela Andreasen Cowperthwaite**

"I love your new O M Gee Instant Pot book - thanks so much for putting all of your fun and yummy recipes together in one place for us all! You da BOMB, Jill!" —**Loyda Frankhouser**

"Thanks a million, Jill, for your MOST AWESOME new cookbook!!! I ready every last word in it, was totally entertained, and can't wait to start cooking from it! You really outdid yourself. It looks like a labor of love. Nom, nom." —**Karen Franks**

"Can I just say, my favorite part of this book so far is the pic to clarify what covering with 2 inches of water should look like. Hahahaha. I love it! Also, I might never stop eating bbq lentils on potatoes because of this book. Mmmmmm!" —**Julie Joyness**

"Your new cookbook is freaking awesome! So excited to try all the recipes! Thanks for doing what you do." —**Ann Duggins Lee**

"Today I downloaded Jill McKeever's vegan, oil free cookbook for Instant Pot's. It is awesome. Most of my veg friends have seen her on YouTube. She is as entertaining in print as she is on the set! Very well written and user friendly! I highly recommend this e-book!" —**Flossie Nichols**

Dear iPot brothers and sisters,

THANK YOU, THANK YOU for making this book a part of your cookbook obsession, uh I mean, collection. If you're into watching food porn, I mean cooking videos, you can watch me put all the meals from this book together on my YouTube channel, *Simple Daily Recipes*. If you're not already a subscriber to my channel, you should probably become one today. Like you, I'm obsessed with using my Instant Pot® and I take every opportunity I find to convert stovetop recipes into plant-based, oil-free Instant Pot® videos. You don't want to miss out on new recipes, plus folks say I'm pretty funny and inspiring. You can turn to me for a lift in your day. ;D

Please read through the entire book, particularly the pages before all the recipes. I know how bad you want to jump to the good stuff, but do me this solid and read the pages before the recipes for me so I can sleep at night. Thank you.

If you have any questions or you want to rave about a meal you made from this book, or you feel overwhelmed to tell me how wonderful I am, you can reach me through my favorite social channels listed on the back cover of this book.

Thank you for being awesome! Have fun cooking with your Instant Pot®!

Your iPot Sister,

Jill McKeever
((WOOT WOOT))

Table of Contents

A Love Letter to My iPot

Dear Precious,

When I think of the years I wasted learning to cook meals out of heavy pots and pans with that needy stovetop, I feel as if I've been duped into cooking harder, not smarter. Of course, preparing meals hasn't always been tedious. For the past 15 years, I've had your cousin, stovetop pressure cooker, to rock my world and chatter on about the golden days when Memaw cooked with her pressure cooker. We created many meals until you, my precious iPot, came along.

I'll never forget the time I spent stalking you online. I read what others said about you, about your many functions and how fast you could be shipped. I watched how other cooks used you in videos, mostly for pressure cooking. I see now they weren't using you to your full potential. Then the day came when I watched how you made yogurt and I knew I had to have you in my life.

I couldn't stand the thought of others having you while I stood in a kitchen surrounded by appliances that could only do one task. The slow cooker could only slow cook. The stovetop pressure cooker could only pressure cook. The rice maker could only make rice. The yogurt maker could only make yogurt. The stovetop could only boil and sauté. I would trade them all to have you. Thankfully, my birthday was coming up and I knew hubby would ask me what I wanted. Oh the day I took you into my arms, I'll never forget the way you looked with all your cute buttons and your solid body. BABY! I couldn't wait to turn you on.

I have a confession to make. After we cooked our first recipe together, I didn't feel like a "real cook." All you needed from me was ingredients, to lock on your lid, and push one of your buttons. ONE BUTTON? Really? You didn't need me after that. I was free to go and do my own thing. You took care of the cooking and keeping the food hot until I was ready. I seriously contemplated whether I had actually cooked. Some foodies would say hitting a button on the microwave was not "cooking." How was that any different with you? I wondered if the other foodies would respect me as a real cook if we were seen together. Please forgive my silliness.

We've been together a year this August 2015. Happy Anniversary, Darling! I love telling everyone about you and the great meals we cook together. You have brought such happiness to my family and have made it possible for us to do more with our time. I'm obsessed with you and I think about you everyday. I love making videos about you, showing off your wonderful functions, and how you've made cooking plant-based meals more fun. You're such a treasure and my secret weapon against stressful meal planning. I'm so glad you were born into existence.

Happily obsessed,
Jill McKeever

STOP! Before You Dive into the Recipes...

If you have not done so already, you MUST READ the Instant Pot® User's Manual. The best way to ensure a long and happy relationship with your Instant Pot® is to read that manual. Trust me on this one. Also some of the most frequently asked questions from new Instant Pot® owners and old Instant Pot® owners can be answered from the user's manual.

Now repeat after me.

"I have read the Instant Pot® User's Manual and found the cooking charts in the recipe booklet that came with my Instant Pot®. I will keep them, along with Jill's O M Gee Good! Instant Pot® Meals, Plant-based, Oil-Free cookbook, with my other worthy cookbooks. I too need the Instant Pot® in my life. Because I like to Rock-and-Roll all night and party every day, my rockstar life leaves me little time to cook healthy meals. Jill, you are awesome. You crack me up and I am or will become a devoted subscriber to your YouTube channels."

Signature_____ Date_____

A Quick Glance at Ingredients
You May Not Have Used, Yet

First let me say, I am not the kind of cook who likes using hard-to-find overpriced ingredients in my cooking. Typically, I say "If I can't get it from the grocery store down the street, I don't need it in the first place." Most of the time, this standard of shopping works me. However, there are three food items I enjoy so much I find them worth hunting down.

Better Than Bouillon

It's a broth base used for making broth. One teaspoon base mixed with one cup of water and SHAZAM, you have one cup of broth. The brand can be found in most all grocery stores. However, their vegan broth bases, No-Chicken base and No-Beef base are trickier to find but worth searching out. I have ordered them online from Vitacost.com but had to make a large order to score free shipping. In my offline foodie explorations, I've learned that not all foodie mart chains carry the same choices. I advise you to ask your favorite grocer who already carries Better Than Bouillon to order the No-Chicken and No-Beef bases for you. The brand also carries a Mushroom base, but be warned, it has whey in it.

Soy Curls

Strange name, terrific whole food. Soy curls are non-GMO, no-pesticides, whole soybeans that have been boiled then stirred until they have elongated into chewy, protein strands. They are then dehydrated and bagged. All we have to do is rehydrate them in water, broth or liquid marinade for 10 minutes then they are ready to eat. Yes, we can eat them freshly rehydrated or cook them up in an old favorite recipe that calls for chicken, pork or beef. Their texture, whether whole, chopped, or shredded will fool even the biggest carnivore into thinking they are eating meat. Soy curls don't have a distinct flavor of their own. The taste of meat comes when we cook the soy curls in the spices, herbs or marinades we associate with a particular meat or dish. I get the best price on soy curls when ordering directly from the makers, ButlerFoods.com. I started out ordering 6 bags then after I learned how much my family loved them, I went back and ordered the 12-pound box that fits in my second freezer. I now use soy curls as a tool for luring carnivores to the Plant Side.

Liquid Smoke

Just like it sounds, it's a chilled liquefied smoke from heated wood chips. There's nothing synthetic about it and it's not made from chemicals. My go-to brand is Colgin Liquid Smoke; comes in Hickory, Mesquite, Pecan, and Apple flavored. You can find it any grocery store. Look for it around the barbecue bottles and marinades. They're totally affordable, so buy one of each flavor. I like to use a couple of drops of Pecan or Apple smoke in cold pasta salads and light soups. For making tempeh bacon, pinto beans, and marinades, I reach for Hickory or Mesquite to get the party started.

Instant Pot® Function Keys
Used in this Book

Looking at the Instant Pot® with all its function buttons can give some folks the feeling that cooking is made easier with a push of a button. As for others, multiple buttons can be overwhelming and confusing. Take a breath. There are four cooking functions I most commonly use. Let's go over those functions.

The Most Important button is "Keep Warm/Cancel"
When the Instant Pot® is being programmed or any program is in effect, pressing the Keep Warm/Cancel button will cancel the program and take the cooker to a standby state. When the cooker is in standby state, pressing this button activates the keep-warm program.

Sauté
Sauté is used for open lid sautéing, browning or simmering inside the inner pot. When the sauté function is activated, it automatically uses the Normal heat setting. There are three heat settings for the Saute mode: Less, Normal and More. Think of them as you would stovetop heat settings, low, medium and high. The "Adjust" button is used to adjust the heat settings, keep pressing Adjust until the light is on the heat setting you need.

Manual
Manual allows manual setting of pressure cooking time. Pressure cooking time begins to count down when working pressure[1] is reached. Anytime you need to pressure cook a vegetable, layered meal, rice, or soup, push the Manual button to start the ball rolling. The manual function automatically sets the timer to 30 minutes using High Pressure. You use the [-] or [+] buttons to change the cooking time. All the recipes in this cookbook will use High Pressure for pressure cooking.

Slow Cook
Slow Cook mode allows you to use your Instant Pot® as a common slow cooker. You can change the cooking duration by pressing the [-] or [+] key between 30 minutes to 20 hours. Use the "Adjust" button to adjust the heating level as in traditional slow cookers.

---

1   Specifications on pressure and cooking temperatures can be found in the Instant Pot® User Manual.

Pressure Release Methods
& Safe Lid Opening

(Just in case you haven't read the Instant Pot® user's manual in its entirety,
which you said you did on page seven.)

1. Make sure the pressure cooking program has completed or press "Keep-Warm/Cancel" to terminate the program.

2. Releasing pressure is done with one of the following methods.

    ### Quick Release:
    *   Slide the steam release handle to the "Venting" position to let out steam until the float valve drops down.

    ### Caution:
    *   Please keep hands and face away from the hole on the top of the steam release handle when using Quick Release. The escaping steam is very hot and can cause scalding.
    *   Never pull out the steam release handle when it is letting out steam.
    *   Please be aware that Quick Release is not suitable for food in large liquid volume or with high starch content (e.g. porridge, rice, sticky liquids, soup, etc.). Food content may splatter out with steam. Use Natural Release instead.

    ### Natural Release:
    *   Allow the cooker to cool down naturally until the float valve drops down. This may take 10 to 15 minutes after cooking is finished and the cooker is in Keep-Warm mode.

3. Open the lid. Hold the lid handle, turn the lid counterclockwise to the open position, and lift the lid up to open. To avoid vacuum suction on the lid, turn the stream release to "Venting" position to let in air when lifting the lid.

    *   **Caution:** Do not open the lid until pressure inside the pot is completely released. As a safety feature, until the float valve drops down, the lid is locked and cannot be opened.
    *   If the float valve is stuck due to food debris or stickiness, you can push it down with a pen or chopstick when you are certain the pressure has been released by moving the steam release handle in the venting position.

O M Gee Good!
Instant Pot® Meals,
Plant-Based & Oil-Free

FINALLY.

Austin Curly Stew

This is my old Texas Chicken Chili recipe from back in the day turned vegan and with a little hot green curry paste stirred into the mix. With all those beans, chewy shredded soy curls, and sweet corn in spicy broth, it has quickly become one of our new favorite meals.

Makes 6 servings

3 cups rehydrated soy curls, shredded or chopped

1 tablespoon chili powder

2 teaspoon garlic powder

1 1/2 teaspoon ground cumin

2 cups vegetable broth

1 (26-ounce) can kidney beans, rinsed & drained

1 (15-ounce) can black beans, rinsed & drained

1 (15-ounce) can diced chipotle tomatoes*

2 teaspoons hot green curry paste

Press [Sauté], then [Adjust] heat to Less heat setting. Add soy curls, chili powder, garlic powder, 3 tablespoons vegetable broth and simmer 1-2 minutes. Add in remaining ingredients and stir together. Simmer for 15 minutes. Press [Keep Warm/Cancel] button twice to activate the Keep Warm mode. Cover with lid. Serve whenever you're ready to serve.

Awesome Tex-Mex Lasagna Stack

Fan Rave! *"WOW.....JUST WOW!!!!!!! I made this and it has to be the best thing I have eaten since my transition to the vegan lifestyle." ~Sandra W.*

Makes 8 servings

16 corn tortillas

2 cups vegan cheese, homemade cheese sauce or shredded store-bought

1 (28-ounce) can diced tomatoes

1 (10-ounce) can chlpotle seasoned tomatoes

2 (15.5-ounce) can beans, drained, (pinto, black, or red)

2 cups rehydrated, shredded soy curls

1 small onion, chopped

1 cup frozen corn

Preparation note: If using homemade cheese sauce, it helps to have it warm and ready to pour.

In a small bowl, stir the diced tomatoes, seasoned tomatoes and beans together. Set aside.

In a second small bowl, toss the shredded soy curls and onions together. Set aside.

Let's start stacking! Start by covering the bottom of the Instant Pot® inner pot with a thin layer of tomato-bean mixture with juice, this will help to prevent sticking later on. Lay down 8 tortillas. Layer half of the remaining tomato-bean mixture, top that with a layer of shredded soy curls and onion mix, then add half the corn on top. Pour on, or sprinkle, half of the cheese. Add another layer of tortillas and repeat stacking vegetables and cheese.

Cover with lid then turn lid clockwise to lock into place. Align the pointed end of the steam release handle to point to "Venting."

Press [Slow Cook], cook time automatically sets to 4 hours.

Fan Rave! "Oh my goodness, this is a huge hit! I made this tonight for dinner and my non-vegan hubby said "this is awesome". I used my Instant Pot® pinto beans that I make ahead and freeze instead of black beans and also added a little cilantro, other than that I followed your recipe to the T. We will be making this a lot.

Thanks, Linda Hardesty"

Baby Red Potatoes for Snacking

Baby red potatoes have saved me from making bad food choices when shuttling kids to and fro during mealtimes. When I know it's going to be a crazy week, I cook up several pounds of potatoes and keep them standing by in the icebox.

Makes 8 servings

2 pounds baby red potatoes, washed

1 ½ cups water

Place the stainless steel steam rack inside the inner pot. Add potatoes and water. Arrange potatoes to sit evenly inside pot. Cover with lid then turn lid clockwise to lock into place. Align the pointed end of the steam release handle to point to "Sealing."

Press [Manual], use [-] button to adjust cooking time to 10 minutes.

When time is up, press [Keep Warm/Cancel] once to cancel the keep warm mode then wait 10 minutes for the pressure to go down. Slide the steam release handle to the "Venting" position to let out remaining steam until the float valve drops down. Remove lid.

Transfer hot potatoes to a resealable container and chill straight away in the icebox.

You can certainly season the potatoes while they're cooling. Some condensation will build up while stored in the icebox, so seasonings like salt dissolve and are absorbed by the potatoes.

In case you're wondering, those are large beets, quartered and pressure cooked right along side the potatoes.

Potato Snacking and Beyond!
Try these ideas from some very special Simple Daily Recipe fans.

Eating a cold potato straight up is good on its own. However, by day three, I'm ready to take my potato-snacking up a notch. The secret to keeping potato-snacking interesting is to enjoy them seasoned with a variety of spice blends and condiments. Try any of the following blends.

Salt and black pepper - Never underestimate the basics.
Kala Namak and black pepper - You'll think you've eaten the white part of a boiled egg.
Mrs. Dash Garlic & Herb or Fiesta Lime
Organic Ketchup
Vegan Russian Dressing
Vegan Ranch Dressing

Tess Roth, "My favorite things to add to cooked potatoes for a quick snack alone or together are berbere spice, hot sauce, pesto (cheese and oil free, of course), mustard (this is what I use when I'm at the airport, I can grab some from a restaurant once we've gone through security), and hummus. If I'm really busy sometimes I'll keep those individual containers of oil free hummus in the house then I can grab one of those plus a container of potatoes and have a quick satisfying snack."

Shana Brannon, professional chef, "I often cut them up and bake them in with my tofu scramble. I LOVE tofu, and this dilutes the calorie density of the tofu. Another favorite is smashed on a cookie sheet and baked at a high temp. until crispy. Also, thinly sliced and used as a layer on a pizza is delicious. Another unconventional way is sliced as the bottom layer of a pile of nachos instead of chips. Potatoes make a delicious base for any bowl style meal. Just pour veggies, beans, some sauce or salsa over top and devour! With the summer heat I'm eating lots of salads these days and I love them sliced as a component of a "nicoise" style salad, too."

John Winger, "I like the Cajun blend in the PlantPure Nation cookbook for the fries. I just leave out the salt."

Shelley Crockett, "I eat lots of baby red potatoes with curry powder and spinach."

Michelle DeVries-Zahrte, "I had this for dinner last night.. Potatoes topped with rice, lentil taco filling, sautéed peppers and onions, black olives, salsa and vegan sour cream... Yum"

Johanne Goddard, "I like to sauté onion and garlic in veggie broth {and any other veg I feel like using that day- green bell pepper, broccoli, zucchini) when cooked to my liking, add the potatoes and season with salt and pepper, THEN, add a lot of finely chopped herbs of my liking. yummy"

Barbecue Cabbage Sandwiches

Fan Rave! "I should have listened to you! Listen to me people, listen to her! I didn't make enough. My family doesn't like cabbage. I made about 1/4 of a large head. They LOVED this. They couldn't believe it was cabbage. I was wrong. You were right. This is definitely a keeper!" ~InstantCrazy1

Makes 8 servings

1 medium head cabbage, cored, cut into chunks

2 1/2 cups your favorite barbecue sauce

4 - 6 whole wheat buns or hoagie rolls

Press [Sauté] to heat up inner pot. Add just enough water to cover the bottom of the inner pot. Add cabbage and water sauté until cabbage begins to soften, 3 to 4 minutes. Stir in barbecue sauce, continue cooking until sauce is heated through. Press [Keep Warm/Cancel] once to cancel sauté mode.

Toast your buns then fill them with a heap of barbecue cabbage. Serve hot with a side of creamy potato salad.

Barbecue Shredded Soy Curls

I have witnesses to back me up on this. The biggest self-proclaimed carnivores to eat my barbecue soy curls sandwiches could not tell the difference between this recipe and pulled pork or pulled beef barbecue. Don't be afraid of the words 'soy curls'. They will be your next favorite pantry staple.

Makes 8 servings

1 (8-ounce) package soy curls

1 small yellow onion, chopped

2 tablespoons garlic, minced

2 cups organic ketchup

2 tablespoon molasses

1 tablespoon Hickory liquid smoke

1/2 teaspoon ground mustard

1 teaspoon salt

whole wheat burger buns

sweet relish (optional)

creamy coleslaw (optional)

Cover the soy curls in warm water to rehydrate for at least 5 minutes. Drain off excess water. To shred use a drink blender set on the lowest speed. Fill the drink pitcher half full with soy curls, turn on blender for 5 seconds. Check to see that all the soy curls are shredded. If not, run blender on low for a few more seconds. Transfer shredded curls to Instant Pot® inner pot. Shred remaining soy curls, transfer to inner pot.

Press [Sauté], press [Adjust] to lower heat to "Less". Add onion, garlic, ketchup, molasses, liquid smoke, ground mustard and salt to the shredded soy curls. Stir until all the soy curls are coated. If it looks like there's not enough liquid for the ingredients to simmer without scorching, add up to 1/2 cup water or vegetable broth. Cover with lid then turn lid clockwise to lock into place. Align the pointed end of the steam release handle to point to "Venting." Simmer on low heat for 15-20 minutes, stirring occasionally to prevent scorching. Press [Keep Warm/Cancel] twice to activate keep warm mode.

Toast your buns, fill with barbecued curls, a dollop of sweet relish, and a scoop of coleslaw. OooWEE! That's some good eats right there!

Cook's Trick
If your carnivore loved-one has a favorite bottled barbecue sauce, use it over the shredded soy curls and chopped onion, then let it simmer as directed. It will really blow their mind.

Barbecue Lentils

Fan Rave! "Holy moly this was GOOOOODDDD!! loved it, will definitely be making it again, and again, and again. I am trying not to use sugar so I used date molasses and it was still delish! I also added some paprika. GREAT recipe Jill! xoxo" ~Michele Coccaro

Makes 4 servings

1 cup brown lentils (Spanish Pardina Lentils hold up so well)

3 cups water

1 small onion, chopped

1/2 cup organic ketchup

2 teaspoons molasses

2 teaspoons liquid smoke

Place the lentils, water and onion in the Instant Pot® inner pot. Cover with lid then turn lid clockwise to lock into place. Align the pointed end of the steam release handle to point to "Sealing."

Press [Manual], use [-] button to adjust cooking time to 10 minutes.

When time is up, press [Keep Warm/Cancel] once to cancel the keep warm mode. Carefully slide the steam release handle to the "Venting" position to let out steam until the float valve drops down. Remove lid.

Add ketchup, molasses and liquid smoke to lentils. Press [Sauté], then [Adjust] to decrease heat to "Less". Simmer until barbecue sauce begins to thicken. Press [Keep Warm/Cancel] twice activate the keep warm mode.

Serve barbecue lentils over baked potato wedges or as a filler for Sloppy Joes.

Watch Jill pull this dinner together on her Simple Daily Recipes YouTube channel.

Best Cabbage Soup Ever, So Far

Fan Rave! "While this was simmering away I made the BBQ cabbage sandwiches with the remaining half head of cabbage. Wow to both. Thank you for your videos and for making me laugh, every time! I look forward to your new recipes." ~Lauri Hatlelid

Makes 6 servings

3 potatoes, diced

2 carrot, diced

1 celery stalk, diced

1 yellow onion, diced

1/2 head green cabbage, chopped

1 1/2 cups canned diced tomatoes

2 Field Roast Apple Sage Sausage links, chopped

3 cups vegetable broth

1 1/2 teaspoons salt

1/4 teaspoon ground black pepper

Place all the ingredients in the Instant Pot® inner pot. Cover with lid then turn lid clockwise to lock into place. Align the pointed end of the steam release handle to point to "Venting."

Press [Slow Cook], press [Adjust] to increase heat to "More", the use [-] button to adjust cooking time to 2 hours.

When time is up, either remove lid and serve, or leave soup in the Instant Pot® while in the keep warm mode. The soup's ready whenever you're ready.

Bring Along Black Bean Hash

This recipe was born from the need to take a hot meal on the go. The night before homeschool co op, I whip up a batch of hash. The kiddos can easily reheat it and fill their thermos before heading off to school.

. . . .

Makes 4 servings

1 onion, chopped

3 garlic cloves, minced

1 large potato, cut into 1-inch chunks

1 small bell pepper, chopped

1 cup canned diced tomatoes

1 tablespoon chili powder

1/2 teaspoon cumin

1 (15-ounce) can black beans, rinsed

1 cup frozen yellow corn

1/2 cup water

Toss all the ingredients into the Instant Pot® inner pot. Cover with lid then turn lid clockwise to lock into place. Align the pointed end of the steam release handle to point to "Sealing."

Press [Manual], use [-] button to adjust cooking time to 2 minutes.

When time is up, press [Keep Warm/Cancel] once to cancel the keep warm mode then wait 10 minutes for the pressure to go down. Slide the steam release handle to the "Venting" position to let out remaining steam until the float valve drops down. Remove lid.

Serve with your favorite tortillas or corn chips.

Watch Jill pull this dinner together on her Simple Daily Recipes YouTube channel.

Watch Jill pull this dinner together on her Simple Daily Recipes YouTube channel.

Fan Rave! "Just made this tonight! Was super yummy, going into the regular rotation. I can honestly say also this may be a good go to for feeding a bunch of folk who all eat differently. Pot luck, bring along indeed."

~Vanessa Anderson

Butt Veggie Stew

I could have called this "Butternut Squash Stew," but what's funny about that? The recipe itself tastes nothing like butt. Not that I've ever tasted butt. I've never tasted a butt. ANYHOO.

Makes 6 servings

2 cups butternut squash, cubed

1 cup yellow onion, chopped

2 teaspoons garlic, minced

2 (15-ounce) can Bush's Kidney beans in Chili Sauce

1 (15-ounce) can diced tomatoes

1/2 (15-ounce) can chipotle tomatoes

1 cup frozen corn

1 cup vegetable broth

1 teaspoon ground cumin

Place all the ingredients in the inner pot. Cover with lid then turn lid clockwise to lock into place. Align the pointed end of the steam release handle to point to "Sealing."

Press [Manual], use [-] button to adjust cooking time to 12 minutes.

When time is up, press [Keep Warm/Cancel] once to cancel the keep warm mode then wait 10 minutes for the pressure to go down. Slide the steam release handle to the "Venting" position to let out remaining steam until the float valve drops down. Remove lid. Allow the stew to cool 5 to 10 minutes before serving.

Watch Jill pull this dinner together on her Simple Daily Recipes YouTube channel.

Got leftover butternut squash?

Try these delicious ideas from loyal fans.

"For your extra butternut squash you can make enchiladas...add corn, onions, green chilies, and use a Tomatillo (chili verde) sauce to coat the bottom of the pan before adding rolled enchiladas then pour leftover sauce overtop. Bake. Yummy!" ~Valerie Scrafford

---

"I like making a simple meal with Butternut Squash or Pumpkin (after Halloween) and equal amounts of Rice and Potatoes; the base stock is made from Onion, Celery, Carrots, Bell Pepper, your favorite spicy pepper, then add Garlic and spices to flavor. Throw in some green beans if you'd like. I make this in bulk and refrigerate." ~Schpankme Verimuch

---

"The leftover BS could be oven roasted with a sprinkle of brown sugar, a bit of cinnamon and pinch of salt. Seriously good that way!" ~Lyndsey Gunal

Chili Bean Goulash

This a great dish to make on those days when everyone is on a different schedule. You can whip it up in the morning and the Instant Pot® will keep it hot and ready for the rest of the day.

Makes 8 servings

1/2 pound dry elbow macaroni

1 large yellow onion, chopped

1 medium green bell pepper, chopped

2 celery stalks, chopped

3 teaspoons chili powder

1 teaspoon ground cumin

1 teaspoon dried cilantro leaves

2 tablespoons low-sodium tamari

2 teaspoons Hickory liquid smoke

1 (28-ounce) can diced tomatoes

1 (28-ounce) can kidney beans, rinsed and drained

1 cup frozen yellow corn

Start with a separate large pot to cook the pasta on the stovetop as directed on its package. While the pasta is cooking, move on to preparing the rest of the recipe.

In the Instant Pot®, WOOT WOOT, press [Sauté] to heat up the inner pot. Add the chopped onion, bell pepper, celery and 1/4 cup water. Water sauté vegetables until onion is translucent. Add the chili powder, cumin, cilantro, tamari and liquid smoke. Stir and cook spices with vegetables for one minute. Add diced tomatoes with the juice, beans and corn. Continue cooking until all it hot.

The pasta should be cooked by now. Drain. Fold pasta into vegetable goulash.

Press the [Keep Warm/Cancel] button twice to cancel sauté mode and activate keep warm mode. Cover with lid and lock lid into place. Turn steam release handle to "Venting." Now everyone can eat when they're ready and you can move on with your day.

Fan Rave! "Omg this was sooo good, I added some zucchini and the family loved it.

Great recipe." ~Tish B.

Watch Jill pull this dinner together on her Simple Daily Recipes YouTube channel.

Fan Rave! "Love this recipe! Yum yum yum. It reminds me of a dish my husband makes, that his Hungarian mother used to make, involving peppers and tomatoes and paprika . . . and sausage. Maybe I'll try this with Field Roast sausage sometime and see if he likes it. Anyway, thanks for sharing and showing how to do it in the Instant Pot® -- such a help for me in getting used to that miracle appliance."

~Lisa Morgan

Creamed Spinach

If you're a creamed spinach fan and you've missed eating it. You will certainly want to give this dish a try. I found no problem shoveling it in my pie hole.

Makes 4 servings

1 (16-ounce) bag frozen chopped spinach

1 cup silken tofu

1 cup unsweetened plain soy milk

1 teaspoon Dijon mustard

1/4 cup nutritional yeast

2 teaspoons tamari

1 teaspoon turmeric

1/4 teaspoon ground black pepper

Thaw spinach quickly by placing it in a colander and running warm water over it. Squeeze the excess water from it and transfer to the Instant Pot® inner pot.

Use some form of blender or food processor to blend silken tofu, soy milk, mustard, nutritional yeast, tamari, turmeric and black pepper into a smooth consistency. Pour over spinach and stir. Cover with lid then turn lid clockwise to lock into place. Align the pointed end of the steam release handle to point to "Venting."

Press [Slow Cook], use [-] button to adjust cooking time to 1 hour.

Serve hot as a side or if you're a big spinach like me, enjoy a big bowl all on its own.

Fan Rave! "Oh my goodness! Sooooo good! Added artichoke hearts and a few chopped water chestnuts. Yummy." ~Samantha Williams

COOK'S NOTE - If you forget to blend the tofu and seasonings together before adding them to the spinach in the pot, don't sweat it. The dish will look more like soft scrambled eggs and spinach shown here, which is still very delicious. ;D

Creamy Potato Soup

This is the perfect soup to whip up when everyone is feeling laid back and wants a light meal.

Makes 4 - 6 servings

1/4 cup yellow onion, minced

6-7 medium potatoes, cut into chunks

1 cup Better Than Bouillon No-Chicken broth

1 tablespoon white miso

1 1/2 cups unsweetened plain soy milk

Stir the onion, potatoes, broth and miso together in the Instant Pot® inner pot. Cover with lid then turn lid clockwise to lock into place. Align the pointed end of the steam release handle to point to "Sealing."

Press [Manual], use [-] button to adjust cooking time to 4 minutes.

When the cooking time is up, press [Keep Warm/Cancel] once to cancel the keep warm mode then wait 10 minutes for the pressure to go down. Slide the steam release handle to the "Venting" position to let out remaining steam until the float valve drops down. Remove lid.

Use a potato masher or immersion blender to blend the potatoes to a creamy consistency. Stir in the soy milk. Season with fresh ground pepper or not, and serve.

Fan Tip!
"I like to add carrots and celery to mine, it adds more flavor and amps up the veggies. Another great recipe Jill !!!" ~ Janine Curl

Creamy Soy Curls Alfredo

Fan Rave! "Oh my! I am in love with soy curls. I never heard of them until your video. They are awesome. The sauce that you made in this video was awesome. My whole family loved it. So this recipe is now becoming a staple in my home. Thank you so much for making my vegan journey so much easier. I'm a fan!" ~Calin Croga

Makes 10 servings

1 1/2 cups dry soy curls

1-pound whole wheat linguini

1 large cauliflower, roughly chopped

1 cup raw cashews

2 large garlic cloves

1 1/2 teaspoon onion granules

1 teaspoon Better Than Bouillon No-chicken Base

1 teaspoon salt

1/2 teaspoon fresh ground pepper

Rehydrate soy curls in 2 1/2 cups water for 10 minutes. Drain. Using the lowest speed setting, shred with a drink mixer and transfer to a large casserole dish.

Cook pasta in a regular large pot on the stovetop as directed by its package. Drain. Transfer to casserole dish and toss together with soy curls. Keep warm.

While the pasta is cooking, place the cauliflower, cashews, garlic, onion granules, no-chicken base, salt, and pepper in the Instant Pot® inner pot along with 2 cups of water. Cover with a nine-inch lid. Press [Sauté] to simmer for up to 8 minutes, or until cauliflower is tender. Press [Keep Warm/Cancel] to cancel sauté mode.

Use a slotted spoon to transfer the cooked cauliflower and cashews to the drink mixer, add cooking liquid too. Blend on medium-high speed until texture is creamy smooth. The sauce will be thick. Add 1/4 cup water or more to loosen into a creamy sauce consistency. Taste for salt and pepper.

Pour the cauliflower sauce over the pasta and mix until well coated. Serve hot with a beautiful green dinner salad. Finally, holler, "Dinner time!"

Wanna serve Vegan Tetrazzini? Add 2 cups of frozen green peas in the boiling pasta water in the last 2 minutes of the pasta's cooking time. Drain with pasta. Sauté 8-ounces sliced mushrooms in broth then stir into creamy pasta. Top with fresh bread crumbs.
Bake at 350°F for 25-30 minutes.

Watch Jill pull this dinner together on her Simple Daily Recipes YouTube channel.

" Time spent with *Family* is worth every **SECOND** "

Creole Rice & Greens

I lived in house of picky eaters, one doesn't like seafood flavors, another doesn't like spicy stuff. I love it all! This dish helps me get what I want and others can leave out the parts they don't like.

Makes 6 servings

1 medium yellow onion, chopped

1 medium red bell pepper, chopped

1 medium green bell pepper, chopped

3 celery stalks, chopped

3 garlic cloves, minced

4 cups No-Chicken Base broth

2 1/2 cups cooked pinto beans

4-5 cups chopped greens (kale, spinach or Swiss Chard)

3 cups cooked brown rice

1 medium tomato, chopped

Kelp Granules

Creole Seasoning

Press [Sauté] to heat up the Instant Pot® inner pot. Cover the bottom of the inner pot with broth. Add onion, peppers, celery, and garlic and cook until onion is translucent. Add remaining broth, pinto beans, greens, rice, and tomato. Cover with lid then turn lid clockwise to lock into place. Align the pointed end of the steam release handle to point to "Venting."

Press [Keep Warm/Cancel] once to cancel sauté mode, then press [Slow cook], use [-] button to adjust cooking time to 30 minutes.

If you're living in a picky household, too, let everyone season their own bowls with kelp granules and Creole seasoning.

Curried Potatoes & Peas

Everybody loves potatoes, right? To introduce my teen to the world of Indian cuisine, I use potatoes to lure him to the table. Works every time.

Makes 6 servings

2 large onions, chopped

1 tablespoon whole cumin seeds

4 potatoes, peeled, cubed

2 cups canned crushed tomatoes

1 1/2 cups cooked Cannellini beans

1 1/2 cups frozen green peas

1 teaspoon ground turmeric

1 teaspoon ground coriander

1/2 teaspoon dried ground ginger

1/4 teaspoon ground cayenne pepper

1/2 teaspoon salt (optional)

4 cups cooked brown rice

Cucumber sauce, makes 1 1/2 cups

1 medium cucumber, peeled, diced

1 12-ounce package silken tofu

2 tablespoons lemon juice

2 garlic cloves, crushed

1/4 teaspoon salt

1/4 teaspoon ground coriander

1/4 teaspoon ground cumin

Press [Sauté] to sauté onions and cumin seeds in 1/4 cup water until onions are translucent. Add potatoes, tomatoes, beans, green peas, turmeric, coriander, ginger, cayenne pepper, salt and stir. Continue to cook until it begins to simmer, then press [Keep Warm/Cancel] button to cancel sauté mode. Cover with lid and turn lid clockwise to lock into place. Align the pointed end of the steam release handle to point to "Sealing."

Press [Manual], use [-] button to adjust cooking time to 2 minutes.

When cooking time is up, press [Keep Warm/Cancel] once to cancel the keep warm mode then wait 10 minutes for the pressure to go down. Slide the steam release handle to the "Venting" position to let out remaining steam until the float valve drops down. Remove lid and allow the meal to cool down a bit while you make the cucumber sauce.

To make the cucumber sauce, use either an immersion blender or food processor to blend the cucumber, tofu, lemon juice, crushed garlic, salt, coriander and cumin into a smooth consistency.

Serve curried vegetables on a bed of brown rice with a cucumber sauce drizzled on top or on the side.

Watch Jill pull this dinner together on her Simple Daily Recipes YouTube channel.

Cooking for Picky Eaters Tip
Since everyone loves potatoes, add extra potato to a new recipe to lure picky eaters to trying unfamiliar meals. Picky eaters will instinctively go for the potatoes first and get an introduction to the new flavors at the same time. Even if they say they weren't a fan of the whole meal, they'll still fill up on the potatoes. Be patient with picky eaters, they need time to get used to new flavors and textures. If you have a recipe you think to be a winner, keep introducing it from time to time. Those picky eaters might come around; meanwhile, you get to enjoy something different.

Extra Creamy Tomato Spinach Pasta

I cannot wait for you to make this for dinner. You're going to want to hug me after you take that first bite. I accept virtual hugs on YouTube, Facebook, Instagram, and Twitter. ;D

Makes 8 servings

1-pound dry tube pasta

1 cup raw cashews

1 cup plain, unsweetened soy milk

1/4 cup nutritional yeast

3 tablespoons tomato paste

1 teaspoon salt

1/2 teaspoon pepper

1 medium yellow onion, chopped

4 garlic cloves, minced

2 cups shredded soy curls

2 teaspoons dried oregano

1 (26-ounce) can diced tomatoes, drained

8-ounces frozen chopped spinach

Let's start with preparing a large pot for boiling pasta. Follow the pasta cooking directions. Drain. Set aside.

Next, make the creamy sauce. In a heavy-duty blender, blend the cashews, soy milk, nutritional yeast, tomato paste, oregano, salt and pepper into a smooth consistency. Set aside.

In your Instant Pot®, WOOT WOOT, press [Sauté] to heat up the inner pot. Add enough water to cover the bottom of the inner pot. Add onion, garlic, shredded soy curls, oregano and cook until the onion is translucent, around 8 minutes. Add drained diced tomatoes and frozen spinach. Cook another 5 minutes, or until the spinach is good and hot.

Finally, let's bring all this home. Stir the creamy sauce into the spinach mixture, then fold in the cooked pasta. Press [Keep Warm/ Cancel] twice to activate the keep warm mode.

Time to holler, "Dinner's ready!"
OH! One more thing. I wrote that the recipe serves eight, but in actuality it will feed four people who will go back for seconds. ;D

Ethiopian Inspired Stew

Even if you're not familiar with Ethiopian cuisine, don't let that stop you from making this FANTABULOUS meal. Eat it alone or serve it with a crispy green salad with a light vinegary dressing.

Makes 6 servings

1½ cups dried brown lentils

3 large garlic cloves, minced

3 tablespoons tomato paste

3-5 teaspoons Berbere Seasoning

5 cups vegetable broth

1 medium yellow onion, chopped

2 1/2 cups butternut squash*, cut into 2-inch chunks

1/2 teaspoon salt

1/2 tablespoon maple syrup

2 tablespoons pureed ginger

1/2 (16-ounce) bag chopped frozen spinach

Berbere Seasoning

2 teaspoons ground cumin

1 teaspoon ground cardamom

½ teaspoon ground allspice

1 teaspoon ground fenugreek

1 teaspoon ground coriander

¼ teaspoon ground cloves

1 teaspoon black pepper

4 teaspoons red pepper flakes

1 teaspoon ground ginger

1 teaspoon ground turmeric

3 tablespoons paprika

½ teaspoon ground cinnamon

Mix all the ingredients and store in an airtight container in a cool, dry place.

Place all the ingredients in the Instant Pot®. Cover with lid then turn lid clockwise to lock into place. Align the pointed end of the steam release handle to point to "Sealing."

Press [Manual], use [-] button to adjust cooking time to 15 minutes.

When time is up, cancel the keep warm mode and wait 10 minutes for the pressure to go down. Slide the steam release handle to the "Venting" position to let out remaining steam until the float valve drops down. Remove lid. Allow to cool for several minutes before serving.

Serve with a green dinner salad.

*Butternut squash can be substituted with potato without changing cooking time.

Fan Rave! "Just got Instant Pot® and this was first recipe tried. Delicious. i went with 3 of berbere didn't know if i could handle and it still has bit of bite. but over all great." ~729miss

Garlicky Garbanzo Beans & Brown Rice

Fan Rave! "I had never thought to reuse the broth after making beans. Did this and the amount leftover was exactly 1.5 cups and I happened to be making 1 cup of brown rice after that. Coincidence? I think not...that's a sign from the Instant Pot® gods :)" ~Mike Cameron

Makes 8 servings

2 cups dried garbanzo beans

4 garlic cloves

2 bay leaves

2 cups brown rice

1 large fresh tomato, chopped

½ small red onion, finely chopped

1 cup fresh cilantro, chopped

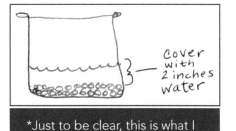
Cover with 2 inches water

*Just to be clear, this is what I mean by "cover with 2 inches of water."

Place beans, garlic, bay leaves in Instant Pot® inner pot and cover with 2 inches of water*. Cover with lid then turn lid clockwise to lock into place. Align the pointed end of the steam release handle to point to "Sealing." Press [Manual], use [-] button to adjust cooking time to 40 minutes.

When time is up, cancel the Keep Warm mode then wait 10 minutes for the pressure to go down. Slide the steam release handle to the "Venting" position to let out remaining steam until the float valve drops down. Remove lid.

Drain and reserve cooking liquid from beans. Transfer beans to a oven-safe bowl with lid to keep warm. Discard bay leaves.

To the cooking liquid add enough water to measure 2 ½ cups liquid. Pour liquid back into empty inner pot. Add brown rice and stir. Cover with lid then turn lid clockwise to lock into place. Align the pointed end of the steam release handle to point to "Sealing." Press [Manual], use [-] button to adjust cooking time to 22 minutes.

When time is up, cancel the keep warm mode then wait 15 minutes or more for the pressure to go down and the float valve drops down. Remove lid.

Reheat beans and serve over a bed of brown rice. Top with fresh chopped tomatoes, purple onion and cilantro.

Fan Rave! "I made this today... you were right about cooking the rice in the chickpea liquid afterwards. The rice and chickpeas tasted so good together! So simple yet so good! Thank you for another great recipe! I liked it so much as it was, just mixing the chickpeas and rice together. I keep going back for more, in fact! :o)" ~Teri Washbear

Just Right Jasmine Rice

Jasmine rice cooks up so quickly in the Instant Pot®. It's my favorite rice to cook when I haven't the time to wait for brown rice.

Makes 6 servings

2 cups Jasmine rice

2 ½ cups water

Place Jasmine rice and water into Instant Pot® inner pot, and cover with 9-inch glass lid. Press [Sauté] to bring water to boil. Press [Keep Warm/Cancel] twice to cancel sauté mode and activate keep warm mode. Do not lift lid. Use the keep warm timer on the digital display to count 9 minutes.

After nine minutes, press [Keep Warm/Cancel] once to cancel cooking. Transfer hot rice to a dish with a lid to keep it warm.

Max's Favorite Mashed Potatoes

Fan Rave! "Your method of cooking the potatoes is great. I also love my Instant Pot®, and all the instructions I've seen involve cooking larger chunks of potatoes on top of the steam rack. That takes a lot more time, and I'm all about reducing the amount of time to pressure cook when it works as well or better." ~2000konnie

Makes 4 - 5 servings

4-5 large Russet Potatoes, cut into 1-inch chunks

1 cup warm, unsweetened plain soy milk

1 teaspoon salt

Put the potato chunks in the Instant Pot® inner pot along with 1 1/4 cups water. Cover with lid then turn lid clockwise to lock into place. Align the pointed end of the steam release handle to point to "Sealing."

Press [Manual], use [-] button to adjust cooking time to 3 minutes.

When time is up, cancel the keep warm mode then wait 5 minutes for the pressure to go down. Carefully slide the steam release handle to the "Venting" position to let out remaining steam until the float valve drops down. Remove lid.

No need to drain potatoes. Use a potato masher to mash the potatoes into your favorite consistency. Gradually add in warm soy milk until you have the creaminess where you like it. Season with salt. Serve hot.

Watch Jill pull this dinner together on her Simple Daily Recipes YouTube channel.

Fan Tip! "I add several cloves of garlic when I boil my potatoes and mash them together then. Soooo good!" ~ Oxana Kabardina

Memaw's Beefless Stew

Do you know the scene in Ratatouille when Anton Ego bites into Remy's ratatouille and is immediately transcended back to the days of eating his mother's cooking? Well, hang on to your tablecloth, this stew comes with a flashback.

Makes 8 servings

8 white mushrooms, quartered

2 large celery stalks, chopped

1 medium onion, chopped

3 garlic cloves, minced

4 cups Better Than Bouillon No-Beef base

5 small Russet potatoes, peeled & cubed

5 small carrots, sliced ¾-inch thick

1 package Gardein Beefless Tips

1 teaspoon liquid smoke

1 teaspoon dried oregano

1/2 teaspoon dried thyme

1/2 teaspoon ground dry mustard

1/4 teaspoon ground bay leaves

1/2 teaspoon salt

1/2 teaspoon ground black pepper

Press [Sauté] to heat up inner pot, then add mushrooms, celery, and onion with enough broth to cover the bottom of the pan. Sauté the vegetables until the onions become translucent. If the inner pot becomes dry before the onion is tender, add a few tablespoons of broth. Add minced garlic, cook one minute.

Add potatoes, carrots, beefless tips, liquid smoke, oregano, thyme, mustard, ground bay leaf, salt, and pepper. Add remaining broth and stir to distribute spices evenly. Cover with lid then turn lid clockwise to lock into place. Align the pointed end of the steam release handle to point to "Sealing" to prevent losing any liquid.

Press [Slow Cook], use [-] button to adjust cooking time to 3 hours.

Watch Jill pull this dinner together on her Simple Daily Recipes YouTube channel.

Fan Rave! "We tried this today and it was great! Even my carnivore husband and 12-year old son liked it. Thank you for another great recipe!" ~ Teri Washbear

Memaw's Soy Curls Pot Pie

I did it! I managed to convert my Memaw's conventionally baked chicken pot pie recipe into a vegan Instant Pot® recipe. Yes, I am A W E S O M E.

Makes 6 servings

Pie Crust (one top crust)

1 cup whole wheat pastry flour

1/3 cup vegan margarine

1/2 tsp salt

2-3 tablespoons cold water

Veggie Filling

1 cup dry soy curls, broken into bite size pieces

1 cup no-chicken base broth

3 medium carrots, sliced

3 medium potatoes, cubed

1 small yellow onion, finely chopped

1 celery stalk, finely chopped

1 cup frozen green peas

1 teaspoon poultry seasoning

1/2 teaspoon salt

Pot Pie Gravy

Remaining liquid from pressure cooked veggies

3 tablespoons white whole wheat flour

1 1/2 cup unsweetened plain soy milk

Season with salt and pepper to taste

Start by rehydrating the soy curls in one cup broth. Set aside.

To make the pie crust, use a food processor to cut one-third cup margarine into one cup flour and a half teaspoon salt. Pulse until the flour mixture has a mealy texture. Add three tablespoons cold water. Process until a ball of dough forms and pulls away from the sides of the processor bowl. Remove dough and roll into a smooth ball. Transfer to a small plate, cover with plastic wrap or damp towel and store in the icebox for at least 20 minutes.

Meanwhile, you can get to work on the pot pie filling. Drain and reserve broth from soy curls, then place soy curls in the Instant Pot® inner pot. Next add carrots, potatoes, onion, celery, green peas, poultry seasoning, and salt. With the leftover broth from rehydrating the soy curls, add enough water to measure one cup. Pour liquid into pot with vegetables. Cover with lid then turn lid clockwise to lock into place. Align the pointed end of the steam release handle to point to "Sealing."

Press [Manual], use [-] button to adjust cooking time to 2 minutes.

When the cooking time is up, cancel the Keep Warm mode then wait 10 minutes for the pressure to go down. Slide the steam release handle to the "Venting" position to let out remaining steam until the float valve drops down. Remove lid.

While the pot pie filling is cooking, get the pie crust dough out of the icebox and roll it out to one-eighth inch thickness onto a floured surface. Work your pie crust on a cool surface or area of your countertop. Measure and cut out the top crust to fit the deep dish, 9-inch baking dish of your choice. With the remaining dough, you will certainly have plenty, have fun cutting out decorative shapes to place on top of the pot pie.

Preheat oven to 400°F.

Back to the pot pie filling. Using a slotted spoon, transfer the vegetables to a deep dish, 9-inch baking dish of your choice. You should have at least one-fourth cup cooking liquid remaining in the pot. You're going to use that seasoned liquid to start the pot pie gravy.

Return the inner pot to the Instant Pot®. Press [Sauté] then [Adjust] to lower heat to "Less".

Whisk flour and remaining seasoned liquid together in the inner pot until there are no lumps. Cook flour for one minute. Whisk soy milk into the flour. Continue whisking until the sauce is smooth and begins to thicken. Press [Keep Warm/Cancel] once to cancel sauté mode. Use oven mitts to carefully remove hot inner pot from Instant Pot®. Season gravy with salt and pepper to taste. If gravy is too thick, whisk in a few tablespoons of water. Pour gravy over vegetables in baking dish.

Time to put on the crust. Top the creamy vegetables with your pre-cut top crust. Use a pastry brush dipped in water to glue your decorative crust pieces to the top crust. Tuck any overhanging top crust into the dish. Place baking dish on baking sheet. The baking sheet catches any gravy that may come bubbling out during baking.

Carefully place the baking sheet with the baking dish on it, on the middle rack of the oven. Bake for 30 minutes, or until the pie crust begins to turns brown along the edges. Remove from heat and allow to stand for 10 minutes before serving.

My Go-To Lentil Soup

I know what you're thinking, "A recipe this simple can't be all that great." Trust me, it's a keeper. The leftovers get thick enough to fill wraps, my teen's favorite food.

Makes 6 servings

6 cups water

2 1/2 cups dried red lentils

1 medium onion, chopped

1 teaspoon dried cilantro

1 teaspoon turmeric

3/4 teaspoon salt

1/2 teaspoon ground cumin

1/4 teaspoon chipotle chili powder

Add water, lentils, onion, cilantro, turmeric, salt, chili powder, and cumin to the Instant Pot®. Cover with lid then turn lid clockwise to lock into place. Align the pointed end of the steam release handle to point to "Sealing."

Press [Manual], use [-] button to adjust cooking time to 15 minutes.

When time is up, cancel the Keep Warm mode then wait 10 minutes for the pressure to go down. Slide the steam release handle to the "Venting" position to let out remaining steam until the float valve drops down. Remove lid. Stir and serve hot.

Fan Rave! "We loved it! I did go ahead and put 7 cups of water in at the start. I made it pretty much the same way you did. Loved it! Easy and sooo fast! Healthy too!! Win, win, win, win! This is a good recipe for someone starting out with plant based diet. There is nothing mysterious about it and it's so easy. :)" ~HoovesandPaws61

Red, Red Lentil Stew

We have Donna from San Antonio to thank for this recipe. She said it was good and thought my family would like it. She was right. This stew is a big hit, with both my family and Simple Daily Recipe fans.

Makes 6 servings

2 garlic cloves, minced

1 medium onion, chopped

3 ounces tomato paste

1 cup dry red lentils, washed

4 to 5 medium carrots, chopped

1 large potato, peeled & chopped

1 tablespoon ground cumin

1 teaspoon smoked paprika

6 cups vegetable broth

Press [Sauté] to heat the Instant Pot®, WOOT WOOT. When the word "Hot" appears on the display, add up 3 to 4 tablespoons water and sauté the garlic and onions until onion is semi-translucent. Stir in the tomato paste, red lentils, carrots, potatoes, cumin, paprika and broth. Cover with lid then turn lid clockwise to lock into place. Align the pointed end of the steam release handle to point to "Sealing."

Press [Manual], use [-] button to adjust cooking time to 15 minutes.

When time is up, cancel the keep warm mode then wait 10 minutes for the pressure to go down. Turn the steam release handle to the "Venting" position to let out remaining steam until the float valve drops down. Remove lid. Allow stew to cool 5 minutes or more before serving.

While attending HealthFest 2015 in Marshall, TX, I met a gang of fans who made this red lentil stew and told me it was "Wonderful!" It was so cool to hang out with them and hug their necks for their ongoing support.

You know you're obsessed with your iPot when you're reading a stovetop recipe and you think to yourself,

"I wonder how I could cook this in the iPot."

Simple Brown Rice

Making a batch of brown rice to go with any meal is so simple with the Instant Pot®. You just have to make the habit of keeping it on hand for quick stir-fry meals and tossing into colorful bean salads.

Makes 8 servings

2 cups brown rice

2 ½ cups water

Place rice and water in the inner pot. Make sure all the rice is in the water, not out of it and stuck to the sides. Cover with lid then turn lid clockwise to lock into place. Align the pointed end of the steam release handle to point to "Sealing."

Press [Manual], use [-] button to adjust cooking time to 22 minutes.

When time is up, cancel the keep warm mode and wait 10 minutes for the pressure to go down. Slide the steam release handle to the "Venting" position to let out remaining steam until the float valve drops down. Remove lid.

Fluff rice with a fork then transfer to a shallow dish with a lid. Serve hot or allow the rice to cool in the icebox, transfer it to plastic freezer bags in quantities needed for future meals. Cooked brown rice can be stored, covered tightly, in a shallow container in the icebox for 3 to 5 days or in the freezer for 6 months.

OH! One more thing. This recipe can easily be doubled without needing to make any changes to the measurements or cooking time.

Slow Cooked Pasta-free Lasagna

You're gonna wanna hug me after you try this AWESOME potato dinner. It is slap-your-momma good. If you've been around me long enough, you know I don't say that very often.

. . . .

Makes 6 servings

1/4 cup cold cashews

1/4 cup nutritional yeast

5 cups oil-free pasta sauce

5 small potatoes, cut into 1/4-inch slices

1 sweet potato, cut into 1/4-inch slices

2 zucchini, cut into 1/2-inch slices

1 red bell pepper, cut into 1/2-inch slices

1 small onion, cut into 1/4-inch slices

2 handfuls fresh baby spinach

1 Field Roast Italian Vegan Sausage link, crumbled (optional)

Using a small food processor, process cold cashews and nutritional yeast into a fine texture. Set aside.

Before you get started, know you'll have enough to make two layers of each ingredient.

Start by covering the bottom of the Instant Pot® inner pot with one cup pasta sauce. Then lay down a thick layer of potato slices, then the onion, bell pepper, zucchini, spinach, vegan sausage, then top with two cups pasta sauce. Repeat the vegetables layers and cover with the remaining pasta sauce. Cover the top with vegan parmesan. Cover with lid then turn lid clockwise to lock into place. Align the pointed end of the steam release handle to point to "Venting."

Press [Slow Cook], cooking time automatically sets to 4 hours.

When the cooking time is up, the Instant Pot® automatically kicks into keep warm mode. Dinner's ready whenever you're ready.

Fan Rave! "This was soooo good! My two children both tried it and really liked it. Then said that they didn't think they would :)" ~Tawni Casteel

Smoky Pinto Beans

Back in my 20s, my Memaw taught me to use a stovetop pressure cooker to cook pinto beans. It was one of the best cooking lessons I'd ever learned. Can you imagine how your grandmother would've loved having an Instant Pot® back when she was raising kids? WOOT WOOT!

Makes 8 servings

2 1/2 cups dry pinto beans, washed and drained

1 tablespoon New Mexico chili powder

1 1/2 teaspoons salt

1 teaspoon Mexican oregano

2 teaspoons liquid smoke

Place beans, chili powder, salt, oregano and liquid smoke in the Instant Pot® inner pot. Add enough water to cover the beans with two inches of water above the beans. Cover with lid then turn lid clockwise to lock into place. Align the pointed end of the steam release handle to point to "Sealing."

Press [Manual], cooking time automatically sets to 30 minutes.

When time is up, wait 15 minutes for the pressure to go down. Slide the steam release handle to the "Venting" position to let out remaining steam until the float valve drops down. Remove lid.

Serve hot over a bowl of rice with cornbread on the side.

Got Leftover Beans?

Leftover beans, kept in a covered container, in the icebox, are at their best for 3 to 5 days. If you're thinking of putting beans up in the freezer, then allow the beans to cool completely in divided portions in airtight freezer containers. Once cooled, store in the freezer for up to 3 months.

Fan Rave! "I think you are great! You taught me what I needed to know... and you are just a beautiful upbeat shining star! Kept me laughing and learning! Keep up your fun." ~Beth Elyse

Spicy Soy Curls Tacos

Fan Rave! "Jill, I made this and it was amazing. My family loved it!" ~ OnMyWaytoRaw

Makes 4-6 servings

1/2 bag (8-ounce) soy curls, rehydrated in water

1 small yellow onion, chopped

1 small green bell pepper, chopped

2 tablespoons garlic, minced

1 (14-ounce) can petite diced tomatoes

1/4 cup Better Than Bouillon no-chicken broth

1 tablespoon New Mexico chili powder

2 teaspoons Mexican oregano

2 teaspoons ground cumin

1 teaspoon pecan liquid smoke

1 teaspoon salt

1/2 teaspoon smoked sweet paprika

1/2 teaspoon ground black pepper

tortillas

1 large fresh tomato, chopped

1 avocado, sliced

Press [Sauté] on the Instant Pot®. Add all the ingredients to the inner pot, except the tortillas, fresh tomatoes and avocado. Sauté vegetables until the broth begins to simmer.

Press [Keep Warm/Cancel] once. Press [Slow Cook], then [Adjust] to raise heat to "More". Use [-] to reduce time to 1 hour. Cover with lid and lock into place. Turn steam release handle to "Venting".

When time is up, remove lid. Press [Keep Warm/Cancel] once. Press [Sauté] to cook out excess liquid in inner pot. Be careful not to scorch the food. Press [Keep Warm/Cancel] twice to activate keep warm mode.

Warm your tortillas, fill with spicy soy curls, top with fresh tomato and avocado.

Spinach Tacos

This is one of those recipes that tastes better the next day. If you can, make the taco filling the night before then put it up in the icebox. Enjoy it for lunch.

Makes 12 tacos

2 large potatoes, cubed

1 (16-ounce) bag frozen spinach

1 medium onion, diced

2 garlic cloves, minced

1 (14.5-ounce) can petite diced tomatoes

1 tablespoon New Mexico chili powder

2 teaspoons ground cumin

1/4 teaspoon chipotle chili powder

12 tortillas, flour or corn, your choice

1 cup Thick & Creamy Nacho Sauce

1 cup fresh tomato, diced

Place the potatoes, spinach, onion, garlic, canned tomatoes, both chili powders, cumin and one- third cup water into the inner pot. Cover with lid then turn lid clockwise to lock into place. Align the pointed end of the steam release handle to point to "Sealing."

Press [Manual], use [-] button to adjust cooking time to 2 minutes.

When the cooking time is up, cancel the keep warm mode. With caution, carefully slide the steam release handle to the "Venting" position to let out steam until the float valve drops down. Remove lid.

Using oven mitts, lift inner pot out and transfer vegetables to colander to drain off as much of the cooking liquid as possible. Return drained vegetables to inner pot. Return inner pot to Instant Pot. Press [Keep Warm/Cancel] twice to activate keep warm mode.

Warm up the tortillas. Fill each with a half cup of spinach potato filling. Top with nacho sauce and fresh tomato. Serve hot.

Tempeh Potato Wraps

These wraps are perfect for a lazy weekend brunch. While the veggies are simmering, toss together a big bowl of fruit to enjoy the whole day long.

Makes 6 servings

1 (13-ounce) package tempeh, cubed

1 small yellow onion, chopped

1 small green bell pepper, chopped

2 large potatoes, peeled, cubed

1 (14-ounce) can petite diced tomatoes with liquid

2 tablespoons tamari

2 tablespoon apple cider vinegar

1 teaspoon Hickory liquid smoke

1 tablespoon brown sugar

1/2 teaspoon ground black pepper

12 tortillas

Place all the ingredients into the Instant Pot® inner pot and give it a good stir. Cover with lid then turn lid clockwise to lock into place. Align the pointed end of the steam release handle to point to "Venting."

Press [Slow Cook], press [Adjust] to increase heat to "More", then use [-] button to adjust cooking time to 2 hours. When time is up, remove lid and give contents a stir.

Warm tortillas. Use slotted spoon to fill each tortilla with a half cup or more of filling. Serve hot.

Watch Jill pull this dinner together on her Simple Daily Recipes YouTube channel.

Thick & Creamy Nacho Sauce

This is my family's favorite plant-based cheese sauce. We drizzle it over our beans, inside burritos and tacos. Over oven-baked fries! On movie nights, we stir spicy chipotle tomatoes into a bowl of nacho sauce for spicy queso dip and over nachos, of course. For cheese lovers who don't really want to give up cheese, this nacho sauce will become a go-to recipe.

Makes 5 cups

2 cups potatoes, cut into small cubes

1 cup onion, diced

1 cup carrots, diced

1/2 cup cashews

2 cups water

1/3 cup nutritional yeast

1 tablespoon Dijon mustard

1/4 cup lemon juice

1 teaspoon salt

1/2 teaspoon smoked sweet paprika

1/4 teaspoon chipotle pepper powder

1/3 cup unsweetened plain soy milk (optional for thinning sauce)

Place potatoes, onions, carrots, cashews and water into Instant Pot® inner pot. Cover with lid then turn lid clockwise to lock into place. Align the pointed end of the steam release handle to point to "Sealing."

Press [Manual], use [-] button to adjust cooking time to 3 minutes.

When the cooking time is up, press [Keep Warm/Cancel] once to cancel the keep warm mode then wait 10 minutes for the pressure to go down. Slide the steam release handle to the "Venting" position to let out remaining steam until the float valve drops down. Remove lid.

Use a slotted spoon to transfer veggies and cashews to a strong blender. pitcher, include cooking liquid. Add nutritional yeast, mustard, lemon juice, paprika and chipotle powder, then blend on high until smooth and creamy. Add unsweetened, plain soy milk for thinning sauce, if you want a thinner consistency. Sauce will continue to thicken with or without the addition of soy milk.

Fan Rave! Terry Brown shared, "This is so amazingly delicious! I loved it as a dip for veggies! I used it as the cheese sauce for a pasta veggie casserole. It is so thick now after setting up in the fridge I am thinking of trying it as the cheese in quesadillas. I will let you know if that works out." One week later: "Ok so instead of quesadillas I made a grilled cheeze sandwich with this nacho cheeze sauce. It was a treat and really easy to make."

Vegan Sausage Scramble

1 (14-ounce) package extra-firm tofu, drained and crumbled

2 tablespoons nutritional yeast

1 teaspoon garlic granules

1 teaspoon onion granules

1 teaspoon turmeric

1 teaspoon salt

1/2 teaspoon ground cumin

1/4 teaspoon black pepper

1/4 teaspoon black salt (Kala Namak)

3 small potatoes, peeled, diced

1 small yellow onion, chopped

1/2 red bell pepper, chopped

6 white mushrooms, sliced

1 package vegan breakfast sausage, chopped

1 1/2 cups fresh baby spinach

oven-toasted tortillas or whole grain bread

In a medium bowl, season crumbled tofu with nutritional yeast, garlic granules, onion granules, turmeric, salt, cumin, black pepper and Kala Namak. Set aside.

Press [Sauté] to heat up the Instant Pot® inner pot. Add one-third cup water, potatoes, onion, bell pepper and mushrooms and sauté until onions are translucent. Stir often to prevent potatoes from sticking to the bottom of the inner pot. Layer vegan sausage, spinach and seasoned tofu on top of hot vegetables. Cover with lid then turn lid clockwise to lock into place. Align the pointed end of the steam release handle to point to "Venting."

Press [Keep Warm/Cancel] once. Press [Slow Cook], [Adjust] heat to "More". Then use [-] to decrease cooking time to 2 hours.

When time is up, press {Keep Warm/Cancel] once to cancel the keep warm mode. Remove lid. Allow scramble to cool 5 minutes or so before serving.

Serve with your favorite oven-toasted tortillas or whole grain bread on the side.

Fan Tip! "Awesome recipe! I did this the extra lazy way and skipped the sautéing step. I just threw it all into the Instant Pot® and cooked it on high for 9 minutes. I did add 1 cup of veggie stock to keep it from sticking, but the veggies gave off a lot of their own liquid so I think next time I'll live dangerously and just omit the stock. The flavor was superb and satisfying! Thanks so much for this great recipe! I know I will have this one often!" ~Teri Washbear

Veggies in Creamy Curry Sauce

Fan Rave! "This dinner is dangerous. It makes you want to keep eating it even after you know you've had enough." ~Charles McKeever

Makes 6 servings

4 cups potatoes, cubed

2 cups carrots, sliced

1 small yellow onion, diced

3 garlic cloves, minced

1 1/2 cups water

4 cups fresh baby spinach

1 cup tomato, chopped

creamy curry sauce

1 cup raw cashews, soaked in hot water, drained

1 1/2 cups water

2 tablespoons curry powder

1 teaspoon salt

1 ½ teaspoons minced ginger

Place potatoes, carrots, onion, garlic and 1 ½ cups water in Instant Pot® inner pot. Cover with lid then turn lid clockwise to lock into place. Align the pointed end of the steam release handle to point to "Sealing." Press [Manual], use [-] button to adjust cooking time to 2 minutes.

In the meantime, make the creamy curry sauce by using a heavy-duty blender to blend cashews, 1 ½ cups water, curry powder, salt and minced ginger to a smooth consistency. Transfer creamy curry sauce to a 2-cup liquid measuring cup. Set aside.

When pressure cooking time is up on the vegetables, press [Keep Warm/Cancel] once to cancel the keep warm mode. Carefully slide the steam release handle to the "Venting" position to let out steam until the float valve drops down. Remove lid. Using oven mitts, lift inner pot out of Instant Pot® and carefully drain off excess cooking liquid. Return inner pot to Instant Pot®.

Fold fresh spinach, tomato and creamy curry sauce into the cooked vegetables. Press [Sauté] then press [Adjust] twice to reduce heat setting to "Less." Simmer just long enough for cream sauce to thicken and spinach to wilt, 1 - 2 minutes. Stir once or twice to prevent sauce from burning on bottom of pan. Press [Keep Warm/Cancel] twice to activate keep warm mode.

Serve creamy vegetables over a bed of Just Right Jasmine rice.

Whole Veggie Pasta Soup

I love how the Instant Pot® allows us to go back to work while a hot meal waits on standby for our family.

Makes 6 servings

2 cups dry pasta

2 celery stalks, diced

1 large carrot, diced

1 small yellow onion, diced

1 small red bell pepper, diced

2 teaspoon dried parsley

1 bay leaf

2 (14-ounce) cans kidney beans, rinsed and drained

1 cup mushrooms, sliced

2 handfuls fresh baby spinach

4 cups Better Than Bouillon no-chicken broth

2 cups hot pasta water

Start by cooking pasta in a separate pan as directed by its package. Drain pasta and reserve 2 cups pasta water. Set aside water and pasta.

In the meantime, press [Sauté] on the Instant Pot®, add celery, carrot, onion, bell pepper, dried parsley, bay leaf and 1/4 cup no-chicken broth. Sauté vegetables in broth until onions are translucent. If the pot becomes dry, add a few tablespoons of broth to prevent vegetables from sticking.

Add cooked pasta, kidney beans, mushrooms, spinach, broth, and pasta water. Season with pepper. Continue to simmer soup using the sauté mode until spinach wilts. Press [Keep Warm/Cancel] twice to activate keep warm mode.

Serve right away or cover with lid and let everyone eat when they're ready to eat.

Pressure Cooking Instant Tips

Instant Tip #1 Half full for beans and grains!

Never fill the Instant Pot® more than half-way with beans or grains and their cooking liquid. They need room to expand.

Instant Tip #2 Don't Spray Foam.

Whenever possible, allow the pressure to go down on its own entirely when pressure cooking beans and grains. They generate lots of foam, and releasing pressure through the valve may spray that foam out. If you're in a hurry wait 10 minutes after cooking time is done, then carefully and slowly turn the steam release handle to "Venting" to release pressure. Turn steam release handle back to "Sealing" when foam exits the pressure release valve, then begin again after waiting 30 seconds.

Instant Tip #3: Don't forget the water.

When pressure cooking vegetables, you need at least one cup of water in the inner pot. Use the trivet that came with the Instant Pot® to keep vegetables out of the water and becoming waterlogged.

Due to the short pressure keeping period for some vegetables, leaving the cooker to naturally cool down without using the steam release will add extra cooking time to the food. For those short pressure cooked foods, it's best to cancel the keep warm mode after the pressure cooking time is finished. Then carefully turn the steam release handle to the "Venting" position to let out remaining steam until the float valve drops down.

Pressure Cooking Charts

Beans & Legumes	Dry, Cook Time (minutes)	Soaked, Cook Time (minutes)
Black beans	25	10
Black-eyed peas	25	10
Cannellini beans	40	20
Garbanzo beans	40	25
Great Northern beans	30	20
Kidney beans	30	20
Lentils, brown, green, red	12 - 15	N/A
Pinto beans	30	20

Grains	Water Quantity (grains: water ratios)	Cooking Time (minutes)
Oats, rolled	1: 1 2/3	6
Oats, steel-cut	1: 1 2/3	10
Quinoa	1:2	8
Rice, Basmati	1: 1 1/2	8
Rice, Brown	1: 1 1/4	22
Rice, Jasmine	1: 1 1/4	4
Rice, long grain white	1: 1 1/2	8
Rice, wild	1:3	25

Fresh Vegetables	Size	Cups of Liquid	Cooking Time (minutes)
Artichoke Wash, trim, and score hearts.	whole	1 1/2	9 - 11
Asparagus Wash, break off tough ends as far down as stalks snap easily. Remove scales if sandy or tough.	whole or cut	1	0 - 1
Beans (Green or Wax) Wash, remove ends and strings.	whole or cut	1	1 - 3
Beans (Green Lima) Wash and shell.	whole	1	1 - 2
Beets Wash thoroughly, remove all but 2 inches of top. Leave roots on. After cooking slip skins off.	whole (2 1/2 inch diameter)	2	15
Broccoli Wash, remove tough stalk ends. Score stems.	whole (1 inch stem diameter)	1	1 - 2
Brussel Sprouts Wash, remove wilted leaves. Cut off stem ends.	whole (1 inch diameter)	1	1 - 3
Cabbage (green and red) Wash and cut into chunks.	2 inch chunks	1	1 - 3

Fresh Vegetables	Size	Cups of Liquid	Cooking Time (minutes)
Carrots Wash, brush or scrape.	whole (2 1/4 inch diameter)	1 1/2	2 - 3
	slices (1/4 inch thick)	1	1 - 2
Cauliflower Remove outer leaves and stalk. Wash and remove discoloration on flowerets.	whole head (6 inch diameter)	1 1/2	2 -3
Celery Separate stalks. Remove tough, stringy fibers. Wash.	whole stalk or pieces	1	0 - 2
Corn (on-the-cob) Remove husk and silk. Wash	whole (2 1/2 inch diameter)	1	2 -3
Greens (Beet, Collard, Kale, Spinach, Swiss Chard, Turnip) Remove wilted leaves and root ends. Wash thoroughly.	whole	1	0 - 3
Mixed Vegetables	cubed	1	2
Okra Wash. Leave whole or cut into chunks.	whole or chunks	1	1 - 2
Onions Wash and peel.	whole (2 inch diameter)	1 1/2	3 - 5

Fresh Vegetables	Size	Cups of Liquid	Cooking Time (minutes)
Parsnips Wash, peel or scrape.	whole (2 inch diameter)	1 1/2	5 - 8
	slices (1/4 inch thick)	1	0 - 2
Peas (Green) Wash and shell.	whole	1	0 - 2
Potatoes Wash and scrub. Peel, if desired.	whole (2 1/2 inch diameter)	2	15
	1 1/2 diameter	1 1/2	10
	slices (3/4 inch thick)	1 1/2	5
	(1/2 inch thick)	1	3
Pumpkin Cut into wedges. Remove pulp, seed and peel.	wedges 2 by 3 inches	1 1/2	8 - 10
	small slices or chunks	1	3 - 5

Fresh Vegetables	Size	Cups of Liquid	Cooking Time (minutes)
Rutabaga Wash, peel, and cut.	cubes or slices (1 inch thick)	1	3
Squash (Acorn) Wash, cut, seed and peel.	cubes or slices (1 inch thick)	1 1/2	6 - 7
Squash (Butternut) Wash, cut, seed and peel.	cubes or slices (1 inch thick)	1 1/2	4
Squash (summer, yellow or zucchini) Wash and cut.	slices (1 inch thick)	1	2
Sweet potato Wash and scrub. Peel, if desired.	whole (2 1/2 inch diameter)	2	10
	slices (1 inch thick)	1 1/2	5
	(1/2 inch thick)	1	3
Turnips Wash, peel, and cut.	cubes or slices (1 inch thick)	1	3

Acknowledgments

I am ever so thankful for the support, encouragement, and love the fans and supporters of SimpleDailyRecipes.com have poured out upon me. You are blessings in my life.

Charlie, you are the most supportive, encouraging and understanding husband a freaking awesome wife could ever ask for. Thank you for being so patient with me.

The completion of this cookbook could not have been possible without the financial contributions from the patrons of Simple Daily Recipes. Thank you, thank you!

Carolyn Ouellette
Loyda Frankhouser
Karen Franks
Debbie Cawthon
Debbie Sanders
Beth Ash
Meghan Quinn
Dar Steinis
John Winger
Anna Filan
Shontae Usman
Janice Tallent
Pat Smith

Kat McGhee
Tara Corbino
Donna Flaherty
Wisteria
Marilea Patrick
Alicia Estrada
Brenda Rawlings
Laura Zimmerman
Bonnie Bird
Kristy Kauffman
Maria Santiago
Tammy Pearson
Andrea Bahry

Travis Posey
Kim Smith
Margarite Olmos
Rene Herndobler
Michele Owsley
Julie Walter
Claire Badcock
Kris Manion
Reina Hamlet
Cynthia Pope
Kathleen Athanas
Cheryl Lemon
Susan Duke

Norman
Ann Lee
Debby Gibson
Suzanne Thurston
Maureen Johnson
Tawni Casteel
Sara Shannon
Vanessa Anderson
Sharon Hudek
Phyllis Mueller
Yvonne Edey
Patty Morgan
Chrystal

Lastly, I want to thank the happily obsessed community of Instant Pot® fans who gave their feedback after trying the recipes in this book and helped make the recipes even better. Also thank you for sharing what your family really thought of the meals.

All together now, WOOT WOOT!

You know you're hooked on cooking with an iPot when you buy one for your best friend then you start thinking of all the meals you could make with a second iPot. When the iPot arrives on your doorstep, you decide to keep it for yourself. (Perfectly normal reaction)

Thankfully, Amazon puts them on sale all the time. Tell your friend to keep an eye out for the next sale, like you did. And it's also perfectly normal to name your iPot. I call mine, Captain & Tennille, because "Love will keep us together!

Connect with Jill McKeever

FAN RAVE! "I have LOVED every one of your recipes we've tried. I actually had my Instant Pot® in the box for 5 months until I found your videos because I was a little overwhelmed with it. I'm not a very good reading kind of person. I really like the visuals. I'm addicted to the Instant Pot® and your YouTube videos now. Thank you so much for all you do, Jill Ann McKeever!!" ~Kirby Colman-Goad

If you are overwhelmed with the desire to support my mission to inspire others to eat more plant-based meals, use the following links to connect with me.

Become a Patron: https://www.patreon.com/jillmckeever
Cooking channel on YouTube: https://www.youtube.com/user/simpledailyrecipes
Live Broadcasts on HangWith: https://www.hangwith.com/user/JillMcKeever
Aftershows/Video Bloopers: http://simpledailyrecipes.com/jillannmckeever
More Plant-based Recipes: http://SimpleDailyRecipes.com

Facebook: http://www.facebook.com/SimpleDailyRecipes
Instagram: http://instagram.com/jillmckeever
Twitter: https://twitter.com/#!/jillmckeever
Pinterest: http://pinterest.com/jillmckeever/

Made in the USA
San Bernardino, CA
18 May 2020

71985304R00053